THIN AIR OF THE KNOWABLE

THIN AIR
OF THE KNOWABLE

WENDY DONAWA

Brick Books

Library and Archives Canada Cataloguing in Publication

Donawa, Wendy, author
Thin air of the knowable / Wendy Donawa.

Poems.
Issued in print and electronic formats.
ISBN 978-1-77131-460-2 (softcover).—ISBN 978-1-77131-462-6 (pdf).—
ISBN 978-1-77131-461-9 (epub)

I. Title.

PS8607.064T45 2017   C811'.6   C2016-907495-1
                                             C2016-907496-X

We acknowledge the Canada Council for the Arts, the Government of Canada through the Canada
Book Fund, and the Ontario Arts Council for their support of our publishing program.

The author photo was taken by Chris Hancock Donaldson.
The book is set in Bembo.
The cover image is by digi_guru.
Design and layout by Marijke Friesen.
Printed and bound by Sunville Printco Inc.

Brick Books
431 Boler Road, Box 20081
London, Ontario N6K 4G6

www.brickbooks.ca

For Leah, first reader

CONTENTS

PU RU PAINTS ZHONG KUI THE DEMON QUELLER ON A MULE

Perilous trip between the underworld and this one.
His mule trots, nimble in a groundless landscape
beneath skies muscled with calligraphy.

Pu Ru's verses explain everything: the insubstantial setting,
the barefoot retainers, one wearing a boot,
carrying a fish and a parasol.

Brushed ink columns, how refined;
I cannot decode Zhong Kui's equanimity
among demons of his world or mine.

Long ago my son, resisting bedtime, said,
The night is a wolf to me.
Dead tree on the horizon, its branches a boney hand.

Perhaps there is only the demonic journey.
Small beauties by the roadside and
such love as we can muster.

Meanwhile the traveller in the tea-gold air
perched on his mule.
Hark. Listen to its trit-trot hooves.

TIME ON ITS SMALL JOURNEY

I
Shelves of clocks and watches.
Neat arrays of miniature tools,
mainsprings and balance wheels, cases and cogs,
like a small herd of ticking creatures
by the altar of Dad's workbench.

All things clockish found their way here,
whether cast-offs or heirlooms.
My earliest grasp of time was quietude,
dim light from street-level window,
overhead light bulb.

I knew to stand still, hands behind my back,
and sometimes he took the spyglass from his eye,
fixed it in mine—
                    I stared in wonder, my small smooth hand
pocked as chicken skin, corrugated scab on my knuckle.

Time scampered through my green years,
my sons and their going; then
galloped through teaching years, each term a tide
of fresh faces while only I seasoned;
paused for an escape into literature,
and for an astonishing late love.
                    It crept
through Dad's long illness and returned me
to a home now strange. My widowed mother, breakfast:
coffee (her silver coffee pot), raisin toast, marmalade. Tremulous.
Each day she wound his clocks, which
whirred and chimed and
cuckooed through the night.

II

But birth and death at once?
Time frozen back in Guyana,
where we, museum curators, gathered
around an Amerindian skeleton:
young woman dead in childbirth,
infant stuck in her pelvis.

Imagine.
See her step, soft-footed, into the bush,
digging stick in hand, cassava basket full,
perhaps before those caravels arrived
cargoed with disease and slavery. Bird-voices of girls,
faces adorned with red ochre. Black fall
of her hair, belly burgeoning.

Terrible, terrible, that we gaze and chat.
We should not be here.
Forever wilt thou love and she be fair. Not here. Forever
will she flex and strain, forever wrench and labour.
Always the child on its small journey.

STONE'S DEEP ACCORD, ITS STEADY PRESENCE

Snow on stone. One crystallized
for seconds, one for eons;
their specific gravities meet.
Snow smokes over elk pastures,
the blaze and splatter of late aspens sloping
through the evergreen of lodgepole pine, of spruce
carpeting ancient inland sea floors
now draped above valleys.

Reefs—
crenellated sawback
dogtooth, lace—
pouring scree down cross-hatched gullies,
sending shale, sandstone, limestone,
spilling this chert, cousin to flint, to chalcedony.
And slate—shale's bastard progeny—fine-grained,
foliated, its fossils' traces
measuring Earth's time scales.

Compressed for millennia
by time's upheavals; striations
sent thundering down the tilt
of layered shelves, oystered in glaciers,
cobbling waterways that loop the continent.
Erosion's runes inscribe its journey.

Stone's deep accord, its steady presence
woven into the world's fabric of being.
Now grounded, stone as witness, as clarification.
Starlight glazes stone with tranquility.
Sun traces it with shadow.
Rain's fingers slick it smooth.

And oh the snow, webbed from air's nothingness:
Its drift, its soft insistence,
its crystal facets scattering light
while days open and close,
folding into the dark.

ABOUT THE SNOW QUEEN:
A QUESTION FOR HANS CHRISTIAN ANDERSEN

A girl shuts the door, tiptoes into the world,
leaves the walls of her life, sun on the geraniums.
So the story goes.
Nothing has prepared her
for the wind-blasted fields, the river's surge,
herself mirrored in the dark unruly robber-girl,
surrender to the wise beast, her face in his rough pelt.

But how to track that regal sled
hurtling through the night,
snow swarming like white bees,
wolves' shadows skimming the drifts,
doors of solstice creaking open,
solar winds flung across the stars?

What tenacity, her small form
clinging to the reindeer's back!
What grasp, her love against the vortex
of the Snow Queen's will, her glacial embrace,
his willing swoon,
thrilling terror of surrender.

And then to find him amid ice floes,
journey's end
in his blank unloving eyes.
Her tears thaw shards in his heart,
the power of innocence ascendant. So goes the tale.
A reverse journey then: faithful beasts, wise crones,
the robber-girl on her fine stolen steed.
Finally the village in spring bloom, grandmother sitting in the sun.

Did the rescued boy close his eyes against this walled life,
sun's glare a scarlet map on his eyelids?
Did he dream return to icy infinities,
to shuddering raptures in the Snow Queen's arms,
magnetic curtains of indigo and green
hissing and swishing across the sky?

TRAVELLING LIGHT

Abandon toppling crates of books.
        I let words slip along my veins,
          rush through arteries in baroque confusion,
          sometimes washing out the heart.

★

Jettison the pottery collection.

Wondrous how the hand spins earth through fire,
and one small bowl fills my palm utterly,
sides an eggshell curve.
My fingers read its stillness.

How to travel without beauty?
I walk carefully, its weight light on my head.

★

Shelved on my tympanic membrane,
stacks of Bach's cello suites
and k.d.'s *Hymns* for nostalgia.

I recall faint clamour
of cocks and pariah dogs in the dim town,
          stars paling in the equatorial night and its tunnelled pain, and
          my new boy soft-skinned, mewing on my belly.
          His petal hands.

I can easily carry that small heft
and knit it down my brain stem.

★

Waking, you warm at my back,
the far escarpment's indigo shadow
and first rays' saffron threading its edge.
Shadows adhere: sour clichés,
        lies, betrayal, tears, all that
        tangles in the gold,
        quickens synapses—systole, diastole—
        pulsing down the rivers of my body.

COMING DOWN THROUGH ROCKFALL

I
I did not guess my tethered life
would loosen to this prairie winter.
A tilted sun flashes the dashboard,
slants the bleached morning
through a scrimshaw of fence posts,
stretches to the edge.

Intaglio of roadside reeds and brambles
tells me nothing;
unscrolling barbed-wire fences are not instructive.
I drive south,
an icy scatter of gravel
the moving centre of this unpeopled world.

II
Leaving early for the Coast, racing daybreak,
I drive with Pergolesi going full blast
till sun sluices down the huge pale sky.
Light spills over fields flat as dinner plates,
snags on stubble.
Westward, winter peaks pierce the horizon, rise
and rise, splintering the sun's flare
till it's all one, that blazing scroll of light, my hands on the wheel,
a silver soprano thread.

A cattle liner trundles past, metal sides clattering,
dense with swaying cattle-bodies.
I know
that always
we lurch toward the charnel house,
and I know

that often
air fills with light and
sometimes the heart with music.
That the magpie plunges, flashing black and teal in the sun.

III
Starting before first light
as dark unpeels itself
from witnessing trees,
from the calm shelf of the lake—
something strange ahead on the road, moving,
shaped like a stag's head; a rack noble with points
but disembodied,
emerging from beneath the earth.

Truck parked askew on the verge, a man
approaching the beast. Something heavy in his hand.
Deer's forequarters struggling, hindquarters truck-flattened,
and the trees lovely in the morning mist,
and grass webbed delicate as insect wings.

IV
The high pass was still icy. Coming down
through rockfall and snowmelt torrents
past ravens cruising roadkill
to the valley. The river high and surging
past green froth of new aspen
to marshes, mauve-grey rushes, and the redwing's trill
stitching the world's tender skin.

THE LAW OF FALLING BODIES

Fire, I think, bushfires. Smoke puffs blue above friable cliffs, then
scree slides, boulders in seeming slow motion,
out of sync with the crash and roar
like a bad long-distance connection. Slide and jostle
on the clifftop: a house-sized chunk tumbles,
its tide of sound
rushing up the ear canal.

A province away, sister-poets
gather in your orchard, crabapple trees
clenched on fibrous roots,
trunks twisted and gestural as the Rackham illustrations
of my childhood fairy tales.
                    Even Sappho urged Aphrodite,
                    Come to this sacred place.
Perhaps you balance atop
a sturdy ladder, anchor one hand
on a lichened branch; with the other
pick and toss to lifted baskets,
your dark hair tousled, cheeks flushed, smiling
at upturned faces dappled
by the turning season's light.

According to the equivalence principle,
both objects fall in the same way:
crabapple with its Newtonian plunk
rolling a little through weedy grass;
torn-off cliff's edge
like a huge pie crust.
Gravity does not equivocate, simply attends to falling bodies;
keeps earth in its orbit,
keeps rivers coursing down their beds.

Later you hover by a large pot, stirring.
Clove, cinnamon,
your forehead damp at the hairline.
By the door, murmur of late bees and women's voices,
windowsill bright with glass jars glowing rose and honey,
ruby, carnelian, amber in the last light.

EXPULSION FROM THE GARDEN

We were war babies, my cousins and I.
We lived on the same street
and had identical twin mothers.
If you needed commiseration,
Ovaltine, or a hug
and couldn't find your own mother,
there was always a smiling double.

The fathers were away, and brave.
Each week the mothers wrote letters.
The older ones who did joined-up writing
wrote *Daddy we miss you*
and we wrote *XXXX* at the bottom.
We trooped to the mailbox,
squabbling over who got to stand tiptoe
and drop letters through the slot.

The hall cupboard was our cave.
We hunkered down in the dark
to giggle and whisper secrets,
and the big ones told us rude words.
Sometimes the mothers called,
What are you up to—
in case we were playing doctor.

Then, into our lives thundered
huge strangers with scratchy chins
and thumping footsteps.
We must never disappoint them.
We had to stay in our own houses
as if there was only one mother.

We huddled in the cupboard to debrief.
When it opened, the shaft of light
a sword across our puppy-bodies.
Rough hands hauled us out
and there were smacks.
Even the big ones snivelling.
The mothers' whispery voices went on tiptoe
when the fathers said, *These children
are getting out of hand.*

And we agreed, the cousins and I,
we liked it better in the war.

AT THE BARBADOS MUSEUM

I. Diaspora's Children

A giant sandbox tree shushes in the breeze,
scatters light and shadow through the courts
where once men were set to breaking stones,
were flogged and hanged.
Long narrow wings of galleries slumber,
sun-warmed; mossy bricks two centuries old
edge the quadrangle.

A military prison, its bricks ballast
from Brittania's ships. Softened with age,
it now charms tourists, offers respite from the heat,
displays artifacts so elegant you want to stroke them:
mahogany hand-honed, satin-smooth
under candelabras with flower-like reflected flames.

In adjoining galleries,
accounts and ledgers from plantation days.
Meticulously kept, they note thus-and-so-many
hogsheads of provisions, rum, salt fish, sugar.
The ledgers of this prosperous planter's workforce,
many-columned: male and female, age and function.
Columns too for Black or Mulatto,
for Creole, African (survivors of the middle passage, of whom
another third still died through "seasoning"—
better to invest in Creole-born stock,
hardier, perhaps beyond despair).
Those under six not yet classed for labour.
Few past their thirties. Through wit or whimsy
given names like Scipio, Caesar, Pluto.

It's a big ledger.
Elaborate script in copperplate
records it all. Sunburned tourists say, *What a shame*
they don't teach handwriting any more.
      Schoolchildren visit. Diaspora's children.
They murmur, lean their soft faces against the glass.

II. A Slave Child's Unquiet Spirit Observes an Archaeological Team Exhume Her Remains

Her restless spirit sprawls across the body.

Had they buried her head to the east, to Africa, her spirit
might have skimmed the ocean, winged home across the salt winds.
Never mind her mother'd buried the navel-string, tethering her near,
tethering her soul where she curls, buried
all widdershins in the slave cemetery.

But she knows she was beloved, remembers
lullabies, Anansi stories, scraps of salt fish, scrapings of molasses.
Hidden in her mother's apron, survival:
women wailing grief
for children sold like flocks of sheep.

Relentless rhythms—sow and glean—
harvests not her own.
Famine seasons, slave rations frayed
till her small bones shrunk with wanting
under the high sun.
And her place in the unmarked grave
through dark and light, through seasons, as drought and deluge
spin the century away.

She waits and listens,
her mother's voice long gone,
        as grave becomes grazing land, becomes cane field, becomes
        parking lot.

Hears clunk of shovels, then
more cautious scrape and brush and
looks up through thinning layers of turf and marl and clay
to faces astonished
by delicate finger bones, by blue beads stringing rachitic ribs.

The spectral child hovers, tremulous—how carefully, how tenderly
they gather her bones, name and house them. At the museum
she stares at her self behind glass:
now data, now artifact.
But nothing replicates sharp grasses slashing her shins,
weighted baskets that bowed her legs,
teeth that show, like tree rings, the famine years.

III. Legacy

White-gloved in the archive, I thumb through manumission records.
Crackle of brittle parchment.
Occasionally slave owners freed their own children,
attested their warm flesh, their smooth skin, to be fully human.

★

Fore-day morning. The planter's daughter yawns, elbows on bedroom
    windowsill.
Egrets cruise the mangrove swamp past sloping fields,
        cane-tops like needles afire with first light.
Soon, clang of cutlass on cane-stalks,

morning's sudden blaze,
        air's molasses-heavy smell.
Downstairs, Cook hums, grating chocolate for breakfast,
and soon the new young housemaid's soft knock. She moves
        to lift her mistress's heavy hair,
        plaits it carefully.

Two girls mirrored. Their twin eyes meet.
Sun streams, stripes their identical faces.

★

Next generation the family leaves plantation life, moves to Port of Spain:
        crocodile of starched

children to Sunday Mass,
        then home to callaloo, fried chicken, pelau.
        Naps behind closed louvres. Parents' locked door.

The eldest girl relishes town life, hucksters' street-cries,
        convent school's decorum,
        forbidden road cricket with urchins.
Her father, of course, has outside children.
        Asks if she has old schoolbooks for a girl her age.

        She says, *You can't give her second-hand books!*
        He says, *Why not, she's a second-hand child.*

★

In the archive, humidity control hums.

WRITING INTO SOLSTICE

Night hunkers down, presses the pine window frame, its uneven caulking.
Misted panes double the murmuring room,
reflect durable wooden tables waiting
      for those who will or will not arrive,
mirror the ceiling lamps into darkness
      across the stubbled slope to the bay.

Through glass, the phantom paper gleams.
The woman fidgets, crumples a sheet, is still again.
Poem or crumpled draft, the table receives them equally.

From other rooms, indecipherable laughter.
Somewhere a fireplace, a log splitting.

THIN AIR OF THE KNOWABLE

Suddenly the bright smell of apples
has dredged up a late night, rain,
and tears for a perfidious lover.
Why that night, those tears?
Why not a spangle of apple blossoms?
Why not polished harvest pyramids
of Galas, Granny Smiths, Gravensteins?

A whiff of hay bales at the farmers' market
returns me to a friend's barn,
lanolin thick on my hands,
hauling pungent fleeces
and stuffing them in sacks, laughing
as the naked sheep circle us
and stare in mild consternation.

What gravitation pulls open
the senses' trap doors,
impels perceptions to the wordless deep?
What clutches those reverberations,
draws them up
to the thin air of the knowable?

Intention does not have the final say.
In the capacious heart
a great silence. The ineffable moves
and is replenished.

From the pond's murk
the carp's slow surge,
grace and glister.
Its sun-spattered fin.

AQUATIC

Somewhere within us fins and tails still flick.
Somewhere an angel struggles to be born.
      —P. K. Page and Philip Stratford, *And Once More Saw the Stars*

Early swim, a few day-blind stars still float the pool's high windows.
A little water slaps the tiles, drums my ears' hollows.

What manner of speech addresses the body, its emptied mind,
its wordless accord with an amniotic world?
What older pulse flows through limbs, kinetic, preconceptual,
slips backwards through its animal essence, back past primate,
to pure vertebrate being, weightless?

An arrow of clear self slipstreams the surface
and water ribbons across back, haunches,
flicking feet;
iPhones, umbrellas, toast for breakfast
sliding away, sliding away, cupped hands
reaching and pushing.

Pure rhythm of body, rhythm of breath, heartbeat,
foundational drum, its cadence and prosody
passing from one medium's density to another's,
refracted. Just so, the swimmer and the swimming, torqued
by warp and crimp of light, of depth,
like metaphor's refraction, magnifying, light-splitting, altering
dimensions and distances. Scattered threads of light
tremble the walls.
Do not believe the evidence of your eyes.

How to translate that phantasm, din of heart and breath in ears;
how turn and return, how mark echo and boundary?
How to craft the mind's movement in language
when the burdensome body returns to the weighty world?

LIFT TIGER TO MOUNTAIN

That tiny bundled woman I saw in Chinatown
sorting through baskets of bok choy
has joined my tai chi class.

She moves to a corner.
Her small hands rise like a conductor's, and
our fumbling vanishes into attentiveness.

Bright as a herring, she pivots
        and we are a shoal, silver with motion.
        When she Lifts Tiger to Mountain, that heaviness
           settles, is folded in our arms,
        and with her White Stork Spreads Wings
           the air billows beneath us, we become
           those clouds unfurling,
                that slow
                    momentum.

Our bodies' unanswered questions carry us forward,
and as we finish, she smiles, and
we, we are all one smile—
a stillness
        spilling
           into everything.

TIME IS ENOUGH

> *Time is enough, more than enough, and matter multiple and given.*
> —Annie Dillard, "Newborn and Salted"

Time arrested, the nutty kernel secret in its shell.
And prairie burrow, either trap or haven.
Perhaps the marrow, soft and fatty in its boney cavities?
Or should I say, the spikey peach pit of the stalled heart?
Stasis, something diminished, but still
                    time is enough, more than enough.

The coiled fiddlehead unfurls, glaciers melt and
hurtle down riverbeds, a child's soft weight
turns to bone and sinew and denial, and we transport
the day's gleanings into night:
those astonishments of sorrow, of joy.

In the brown shallows at the lake's edge,
three ancient pickerel—as long as my arm!—
scraped their bellies on smooth stones.
Slow arching backs, fins signalling out of water,
a lolling pod of miniature breaching whales.
Their languid progress through bright air,
dappled water, lattice of branch and root,
                    and matter multiple and given.

AFTER THE BIOPSY

The angel of uncertainty
has crash-landed on your balcony
where scarlet flax blades
spike the autumn sun.

He hovers almost glimpsable
from the eye's edge
        till the mind overflows.

Deep in the night
he drifts behind you, nibbles his fingernails
as you stand at the open fridge
spooning yogurt from the container.
        Murmurs something—though you can't quite catch it—
        about how life boils you down to a small gravy.
Won't be ignored, dithers at your shoulder, and
dissolves into the computer's equivocal reflection.
A sour draught from itchy pin feathers.
        He cricks his white knuckles so you jump,
        swivel to catch a random flicker.

Chimera of the dark
        rattling dice and test tubes,
        tap dancing in the shadows.

AFTER A BUSY YEAR, I ARRIVE AT NON-ACTION

Less and less do you need to force things,
until finally you arrive at non-action.
    —Lao Tzu, *Tao Te Ching* (translated by Stephen Mitchell)

Windless river valley
seems primordial, crystallizing air
        at minus thirty.
        Shared coffee thermos.

Sorrow and mystery
of a phantom limb:
        the alienated son.

Young woodworker,
face like a Thai angel,
finishes the desk:
        fragrant cedar, narra.
        Morning light trapped
        in the jar
        of yellow willow.

Mountains away, sheared
car. Your shattered sternum,
my frantic hovering.
        Pain recedes slowly,
        but fear has
        taken up residence.

Mind agitates:
        rethink, rewrite, revise.
August deadlines.
Reassembling tropes

the editor finds
too highfalutin;
        work in pajamas,
        eat from saucepans.

Kayak, a dream
on mirrored mornings;
tai chi tidies
my crumpled days.

The surgeon asks
how I understand
        the meaning of cancer.
The hospital tarmac
steams with rain.
        Gold aspen leaves
        plaster the windshield,
        coins for the ferryman.

They say those unconscious
can still hear you.
        It's true. Immobilized
        by some huge gravity,
        I hear sighs
        and bedrails rattling
        and somewhere deep
        your voice underwater, calling.

Finally float, surface.
Somehow your face,
        my name in your mouth.

UNINVITED

The psyche's bottom-feeders stir, sluggish
while she grinds coffee,
waters the cyclamen.

The day unfolds. Steamed froth
for espresso, unremarkable yet comforting.
Rustle of newspaper.
On the winter balcony
bamboo shuddering.

Then, what urgency enters?
How to welcome the unsolicited?

The axis tilts. Slope of sunlight
splashes the brass healing bowl,
calls up the unresolvable:

        neat rind of the incision, its secret itinerary;
        plastic barrettes for her ninth birthday;
        dental records from her brother's body.

Hieroglyphics of the buried life haunt the quiet room.

Later, her face looms in the night window
and doubled candles greet
what is left, what vanishes.

IN THE GALAXY OF OUR EYES

What we think we see
is the dark noise
of shadow moving behind the gaze.
Small teeth gnashing—
crunch crunch—
under the porch.

In the galaxy of our eyes
the fovea anatomizes detail,
gives us carnivals and colour,
discerns evening light on water,
lamp-gleam on a lover's shoulder,
the last gold leaves flickering on November branches.

To observe a dim star, astronomers avert vision.

Poets approach slantwise,
go by hunch, root for metaphors.
Like mushroom hunters
scrabbling in pine needles for chanterelles.
Peripheral tides bring flotsam:
barnacles and lavender,
dead bees, persimmons even! How
to craft them past themselves?

It is snowing again, dusk dissolving.
Silence so deep it beckons.
Relinquish.
Even the magpie hunched on its perch.

THE PERMEABLE MEMBRANE

> *How could the material world, the world we consumed, claim divinity or even*
> *kinship with human kind?...* Beauty is the permeable membrane.
>   —Sena Jeter Naslund, *Ahab's Wife*

Things for which there are no words.
Daisies the morning after a storm,
tough stems corkscrewed,
white and yellow coronas
flat in the wet grass.
That smell, between fresh and rank—
ironed linen, slightly scorched.

No transcendence
      for the plain chair, the blue bowl of raspberries.

In the muddlesome roads of our dreams
we meet our selves, see how
things might be otherwise, how
metaphor extends us,
invites love for a difficult world,
opens the long bag of our shadows
where the dear dead arise—
not elegiac at all, but practical, opening drawers, leaning against the wall
while we comb out past tangles
(meanings pulling all askew),
tasked to find patterns
in a contingent life.

The dead bee on my carpet
clutches its tiny death
against the patio door
streaming with October rain.
But we can only move through
beauty's membrane, sailing to Byzantium.

PRAISE-SONG FOR JENNY

I stayed in vigil all night,
my hands shaping the gesture of letting go,
watched the thick candle gutter into dawn,
walked the hedged road where homeless men cough and huddle.

My hands shaped the gesture of letting go
by the brick labyrinth under a flannel sky, under the cathedral's high
    clerestories.
I walked the hedged road where homeless men cough and huddle,
walked a maze of memories to their core

in the brick labyrinth, under a flannel sky, under the cathedral's high
    clerestories.
Our young laughter on the hot sand
(we've walked a maze of memories to their core)
where we oiled our enormous pregnant bellies.

Our young laughter on the hot sand
(you moved with the turning earth)
as we oiled our enormous pregnant bellies.
The tjanting you sent from Jakarta.

You moved with the turning earth.
Your Yixing teapot so easy in the palm;
the tjanting you sent from Jakarta
rests solid on its shelf.

Your Yixing teapot so easy in the palm
—the stars quite gone now—
rests solid on its shelf.
The first ray a sunburst in my eye,

the stars quite gone now.
As the wind flickered your bright hair,
the first ray, a sunburst in my eye.
A hemisphere away, your afternoon mourners gather.

Bright as your wind–flickered hair,
the thick candle guttered into dawn. I watched.
A hemisphere away, your afternoon mourners gathered.
I stayed in vigil all night.

ITS INFINITE STARSHINE

Cold enough for snow.
Mottled clouds heavy with darkness.
Silence seeps into corners,
binds sleepers to their soft beds,
burrows into their dreams
so they shift and murmur.

In this high building that
men have made for our stacked lives,
a solitary one pads across the room,
drifts into sudden moon-flood.
Below, cars huddle in silent rows,
streets stroked black and gleaming
by the rain.
Only the traffic light wakeful,
its slow blink in the dark.

In all this,
where is intention?
How does it stand
in these trapezoids
of moonlight parsing the room?
Striped shadows slide along
the rocking chair's ellipse, slice the table,
wind ribbons of light around the porcelain bowl.

Through the window's lens,
all the firmament, its infinite starshine;
shredded clouds and shining streets.
On the window ledge, a black silhouette:
sunflowers in a tall glass jar.

GHAZAL

At least today give me a call
or text or tweet or have a plan.

All night the rain shone black, intrusive
as static on our old phone's party line.

Tomatoes in the fridge gone green and fuzzy,
pure November mouldering.

Every angel is terrible
arriving from the cancer clinic.

Salt spray in my face, a message
I hesitate to unfold.

Was there a time I lit candles for my lover?
Sprinkled cinnamon on her toast?

ON READING P. K. PAGE'S "STORIES OF SNOW"

Night fading, unseasonal snowdrifts
lifting river mist, cliffs dissolved.
Leaving seemed
a dream
of departure.

Next dawn, waking
to a pale ceiling awash
with the absence of everything but morning light.

Strange then to encounter P. K.'s poem:
snow light falling white
among the swans, the drift of their down, and
men in a colourless landscape
who dream their way to death.

I bought these white freesias,
star-bright,
to conjure your face.

MOST WISHED IN HER WILD HEART

Now even the gnarled ginger root
guards its aromatic gift.
Just so, the bone its marrow. And just so
the sun its shadows, swung against the day
as bamboo contours sweep my wall.

Once, a yellow-eyed hawk perched on my balcony.
What it offered I cannot entirely name.

For instance, a row of favourite pots hangs,
a chosen knife waits, quiet and gleaming.
Also, how you sit, chin in hand; how your glance
softens through the stew's herbed steam.

Even violet-haired Sappho
unsure what she most wished
in her wild heart—
but still that loosening of limbs.

KIT KATS FOR THE BLESSED

My beloved lives down the river valley
edged by escarpments wild above wolf willows
and golf club condos.
      Occasionally her neighbour's garage opens
      to an Aladdin's cave of pastel Rubbermaids
      stacked up the walls, mitred into corners,
      even piled on platforms pullied to the ceiling.

The neighbor peers kindly over rimless specs,
has brought us homemade Saskatoon preserves, although
her faith group prescribes stockpiled
food, only for the righteous.

          Come the apocalypse
    all nature will surge and thunder,
      obliterate the godless, while the Saved will open
      their Rubbermaids for canned soup, noodles,
      potato chips of bliss, Kit Kats of the blessed.

Sometimes we joke nervously, *What if they're right*,
remembering last year's floods
that yanked trees from their moorings, swallowed buses
like so much Lego, smashed them into bridges,
swept houses built on flood plains
into the current, like those biblical warnings
against houses built on sand.

      It's hard to believe now;
      the river's sage-and-pewter shimmer
      belies its grip and drag along the continent's spine
      beneath a sky innocent with Magritte clouds.

But a year ago I watched as mammoth chunks of coulee
split and thundered down the cliff, smashed
the gulch, clogging the sky with dust,
rowdy as Armageddon.

And we imagine huddling by that garage door,
scratching for alms under damning torrential hail,
having long scraped out the peanut butter jar
and downed the last of the wine. Might
our neighbour feel
a faint regret
at the plop of Rubbermaid lids,
      glug of water tank,
            crinkle of Miss Vickie's bags,
                  sizzle of deep fryer, and
songs of jubilation as she waits

till the damned are washed downstream and
the cleansed world gleams green as golf courses?

TREATY RITES

I heard on one of those late-night talk shows
that folks in New York sell space above their buildings
but the friend I told said, *That's crazy talk;*
how could you sell air? Just imagine it:
Excuse me sir, you're breathing my air. She went on like
this till I wondered if I'd misremembered.

But it's not so far-fetched when you think of
the Coast's first people. Probably incredulous
at early invaders—the big ships, kettles, axes—
and hornswoggled by the way they did business.

Sometimes I imagine the conversations.
Women padding home through the forest
with berry-filled baskets, or piles of the cedar's
soft inner bark to weave fabric
or fashion elegant rainproof hats:
> *Can you believe those guys? They think the land can belong*
> *to a person. That a person can own trees! Next thing you know*
> *they'll say they own birds! They own berries!*
Laughing so hard they have to stop, put down their baskets
near the longhouse, share the joke with husbands
backing canoes onto the beach—those once-living trees
now flared and sleek, bearing humans between land and sea
and all the spirits there inhabiting.

The men smile too, somewhat uneasy:
> *They're pathetic, really.*
> *But we humour them, make the little cross-mark designs,*
> *say uh-huh, uh-huh to be polite.*

> *Don't suppose they'll do any harm.*

TESTIMONY OF SUBJECT NO. 22

*...an international team of researchers has shown that the bacteria living in
the digestive tracts of previously uncontacted hunter-gatherers [in the Amazon]
are the most diverse yet found in any human group.... In the Venezuelan
study, which involved a genetic sampling of the bacteria found in the feces,
saliva and skin of 34 Yanomami villagers, researchers found genes that are as-
sociated with antibiotic resistance.*
    —The Globe and Mail, April 17, 2015

They came on a day like any other.
The forest with its early morning voices
and the sun not yet in our clearing.
The smallest children on their mothers' backs
or at the breast, and cassava on the baking stones.

We had of course occasionally seen those flying boats,
but at a great distance, and far above the forest.
We thought them perhaps of another world
and nothing to do with us.
Of their landing—its fearful noise, the forest's shredded canopy, our flight—
we have already spoken.

Yet the beings that emerged seemed of humankind,
smiling, hands open in greeting, and
apparently harmless. Their gifts were very fine—
sharp knives, kettles—and we had enough
cassava cakes to share. The small oblong foods
they gave us strangely delicious, sweeter than honey;
in no time, the children laughing and clamouring.

They seemed to lack a layer of skin—
so pale, smelling not quite human—and wore
fragile clothing that covered all their limbs.

It didn't look comfortable,
but you could see they meant well in their clumsy way.
They couldn't talk properly, but we managed with signs and gestures,
told them a few words any child should know.
They did not call me by my name
but named me *Twen-Tee-Tu*.
Perhaps it was a blessing.

A marvel to watch them
unpack their carriers. Many small containers, all the same size.
So beautiful; you could see right through them, like water. I tell the truth.
The tall one painted signs on them as I watched, then
painted the same sign on my arm, said my new name.
He gave each of us a sign, even the children,
a benediction of some sort.

But they did not know how to behave.
Perhaps you will disbelieve me:
they wanted to put our mouthwater and our shit
in their beautiful clear-as-air containers.
The request was so unseemly we murmured
that this is something we do in the forest,
but after all, they were our guests,
so finally we did as they asked, and as I brought mine
to the tall shaman he blessed me, said my new name,
and gave us small tasty many-coloured foods
so the children all shouted and ran about.

They put the containers in their flying boat, and next morning
the tall one held my hand, said *Twen-Tee-Tu*
and climbed into the boat.
We ran into the forest as it made that terrible sound.
It flew them away

and sometimes we wonder if we dreamed a vision.
We wonder if they have stolen our bodies' essences
and if the names were not a blessing but a soul-theft.
I wonder if the tall shaman thinks of me
when he lifts the beautiful containers.
The children are fractious, sulking for small bright foods.
It no longer gives me pleasure to smell morning cassava on the baking
    stones.
The sacred signs have faded from our arms.

RECONCILING THE SQUARE

> *...some skull must rub its memory with ashes,*
> *some mind must squat down howling in your dust,*
> *some hand must crawl and recollect your rubbish,*
> *someone must write your poems.*
> > —Derek Walcott, "Mass Man"

In the South of my circled life, dry season rustled the cane
and bamboo rattled under the moon.
I knew this place, comfort amid discomfort,
though sometimes saw my pale face in shop windows,
a shock—my reflected self as *other*,
history's sins stamped on my forehead.
Then I tumbled into the square of this North
disguised in my fraudulent skin,
rolling up an Ariadne's skein of cause and effect.
> *Some skull must rub its memory with ashes.*

That Russian scientist, the one who made dogs salivate,
conditioned their responses—first to a circle, then a square.
Stage by stage, he rounded the squares' corners,
squared the circles like an old-fashioned TV.
The dogs whined and cringed as shapes became indistinguishable.
Inconsolable, toppled into psychosis.
It was considered an elegant experiment,
acknowledgement that for each quantitative gain
> *some mind must squat down howling in your dust.*

Tuesday is Folding Day.
And afternoon women who once created jewelled shelves
of cherries, jams, and peaches, shouted for late children,
drift toward the Activity Room.
Attendants heap out rumples of

baby clothes across the long table.
The women smooth them flat (because Tuesday is Folding),
stroke out the tiny sleeves
and fold them carefully, carefully
—oh, lovely—until they're neatly basketed,
then wait while the attendants
tip them out again. Oh. Lovely.
>   *Some hand must crawl and recollect your rubbish.*

Spring is late this year. A raw wind and shrivelling buds,
but on View Street the bright scoured sky
judders a foment of plum blossom
over the wild-eyed prophet who trundles on ruined feet
beneath the contrapuntal finches, while
the tink tink of bottles in his shopping cart
heralds his cardboard messages of doom and retribution.
>   *Someone must write your poems.*

LATE AND THE LIGHT ALREADY TURNING

Light spills from winter's icy chalice.
Scrims of snow gather coasting gulls,
shake them out like laundry.
It is a white morning, although darkening days
slant to the year's midnight.
A white morning, it weighs on eyelids,
settles on the red winter quilt.

But earth tilts on the solstice fulcrum,
away from the year's fracking, from renditions,
from Mandela's death and the world's crocodile tears.

Tears, nothing to dementia patients waiting for the bus.
To the mad prophet, sleeping bag jumbled in his cart.
To children trudging rifles through Sahel dust,
indecipherable as angels in the snow.

In Barbados now, poinsettia hedges glow and
the cane is inflorescent, each field a white sea
of plumes stark under the moon.

Did we imagine the brightness of that summer market stall
where two men sold sunflowers? Each week
a galaxy of cultivars—we almost couldn't choose.
Their whorled heads weighty in our arms.
Then one man, alone, an empty chair at his side,
wrapping our Saturday purchase.
He said, *The cancer took him.*
You only find love like that once.

It is getting late and the light already turning.
Still, we attend to white light on a red quilt
as one might keep a smooth beach pebble which,
held, harvests the hand's warmth.

A FIBONACCI SEQUENCE

Try

two

to one:

oil and vinegar,

essential vinaigrette. Of course, best

to use cold-pressed double virgin olive oil and

aged balsamic vinegar. Simple: twice as much bland as piquant. A golden
mean

that in the salad dressing of life signifies twice as much boredom as
excitement. You could add lemon zest, garlic cloves,

cracked pepper, but finding the balance is about accumulation, not
arithmetic. In space, expressed by the nautilus's spiralling chamber,
sunflower's rotary swirl, artichoke and pinecone, helix of DNA,
Leonardo's man suspended in his squared

circle; in sound, how the sharps and flats of Schubert's *Trout* Quintet land
on the heart's surface tension quiet as water striders delicate on slow-
running streams. Nature's harmony arising from numbers; for Pythagoras,
perfection's source. Golden mean: its rhythms unfold seashells, music,
physics. Spiralling on their axis: horns, claws, unfurling ferns, fingerprint
whorls. So

proportion's mystery and mathematics flare, bless the mundane,
illuminate the prosaic, sanctify the plain perfection of Chardin's table,

exalt sunlight streaming through Vermeer's window. Then blessed be the unfamiliar tang of dried roots in the Chinese apothecary's, old women laughing in the bakery, swoop and glide of skateboard boys, stretch and splay of cedars. Consider your coffee's lifting coil of steam, slow disintegration of its vortex, stoneware cup's glaze fossilizing its potter's fingered spirals, tracing its upward shaping. Arcs of spray as you water potted parsley, thyme, basil. Humming.

FEEDING POETS

Picked up my *doro wat* order from the Ethiopian takeout.
Dropped my *Poisonwood Bible*.
Cook from Addis Ababa, he'd read it too.
Confused by its five voices in this his fourth language.
My *doro wat* cools. I explain layers—like flavours.
He gets it.

Later I thought, garlic, ginger, allspice; thought, fenugreek, chili, coriander;
        thought, clove and cardamom;
        thought, berbere.

Monsanto website assures us genetic modification
        will give nature a little boost
        and solve the world's hunger.

Over won tons and tuna sandwiches
a poet explains Schrödinger's cat.
We all admit we don't get it
        although we understand
        the moment that supposition becomes possibility
        is the fulcrum for much poetry.
Don't get string theory or particle accelerators either.
        After lunch, Pam's Mexican Wedding Cakes—
        that sensory *suddenness* we strive for
        in our poems.

Small herd of bison near Chicago
grazes tall-grass prairie over
a particle accelerator two miles long,
                fetches up the God particle,
                suggests divine wrath.
                (Apparently it's deeply unsophisticated

to call Higgs boson the God particle.)
Bite into Pam's Mexican Wedding Cakes—
    silent fireworks of icing sugar,
    tracks to your door.

ON YOUR SURVIVING AN ACCIDENT IN A FAR PROVINCE
THE NIGHT OF THE TSUNAMI

Sleepless again at three o'clock
and back in bed with mint tea
on my quilted knees.
Scudding clouds and patio chairs rattle the night.

I switch on music, hoping for Bach, and hear instead
that a tsunami is flinging itself
across the world to gnaw at our coast,
even at tidepools where fleshy stars
cringe and grasp, then

words scroll across this washboard province,
across its greening slopes, appear blue and silent
on my screen: screech and shear of your collision,
        and my everything races
                to absorb its wreckage,
                        to cradle your origami bones.

HOW IT ALL GATHERS

I should have cut back the grass by now—
blood grass curled, hardened to bronze.
Winter gales funnelled by the balcony,
my eyrie in the salty air,
so small a domain. It occupies me;

I welcome hummingbirds exquisite as *netsuke*
who've found my winter jasmine and
savage the small gold trumpets on its twiggy vines
with their stiletto beaks.

I long for *miyabi*, and yet
mid-winter shreds even the black bamboo's elegance.
Bungee cord the potted grasses,
crop them close, a crewcut row, delinquent boys.

Streaks of scarlet along the sunset horizon
stream the firmament. I don't want to write
about love again. How it all gathers, reflects
in our wineglasses, in your eyes.

AUBADE

In that long twilight before sun-up
grey light seeps through blinds,
stripes my dreams where
lost boys wander the corridors,
surface through light and shadow
until they fade.

Everything aches.
This friendly body, my good animal,
now slow to my bidding,
hatches mutinous cells and clamours for sleep.
Of that coltish girl no remnant,
not even in the deepest mirror.
When did I start to be old?

The sun
stamps its bright bar code on the wall,
and I turn to you
and our late love in these flannel sheets.

What we say goodbye to
—the romp and flex of salad days,
supple muscles heedless of the night—
gives lustre to all that our stitched bodies
have scavenged from a shattered world,
weight of loss and loving.

Somehow catastrophe's patina
glosses our *now* of pleasure:
raku still glowing from the kiln.
        It's not late yet.

LEXICON

When I was eight, I learned
to use the dictionary and earned
brief popularity
from the exegesis
of forbidden words.
I learned to take the bus that year,
to wait at the Fort Street stop
across from the Dutch Bakery.

Beside the bakery, opaque and gleaming, a black glass door
reflected my mittened self
under gold letters spelling men's names,
then *Executors*.
I knew about *execution*,
had looked it up, had perched on Dad's cretonne armchair
where he read the evening paper
while the nation still used the noose
and sentenced fourteen-year-old boys to hang.
Looked up *noose* too. *Garrotte. Hangman.*
Woke shrieking in the night.

Weekly I trembled for the bus.
Once, a duffel-coated man went through that door,
swinging my reflection into the bakery's crusty pastries:
Executor. Executor.

WAITING FOR THESEUS

It suits them well to call me monster,
wall me deeper than the grave
and out of sight and mind.
Father's vengeance, Mother's passions
unspool my forlorn fury.
Bestial power, human longing.

They fling me boys and girls so deft and lovely
it could break your heart. And does.
Desperate dexterity. Their dances
end on my horns. In grief, not rage,
in the desolation of one
alone of his kind, my bellows

reverberate in spirals,
echo through the labyrinth.
                    They've summoned
the seducer now tying Ariadne's thread
to the outside doorknob.

Soon he will come.
If he might bring me apples, scratch my ears,
I could bury my soft muzzle in his hands and weep for joy.
But I think I will welcome his bright axe,
turn my neck to its edge.

THE WINGED BOY ITCHES TO BE GONE

Strung like a bow, Icarus
itches to be gone. Daedalus fusses,
twitches feathers. The winged boy shrugs;

he's heard it all before. He leaps to
flumes of delicious terror, swooping,
strung like a bow. The boy

rides the light, looks down, his bird-shadow
rippling on the corrugated sea. The wind-stream
twitches Icarus's feathers. He shrugs, flexes

the cage of his ribs, holds a wingspan of
desire on the day's blue thermals. Windhover,
strung like a bow, the winged boy's creaking quills

on the membrane of the wind's ear. Below,
Daedalus's cries, the labyrinth's spiral.
Twitching feathers, Icarus shrugs, ignores

his father's dire work, beast-bellows. Gold amid
the sky's blaze, apotheosis. Then no longer
strung like a bow, the winged boy's wax-loosed
feathers twitch, shrug him to the cresting waves.

ON MY BEDROOM WINDOW, FROST FLOWERS

Chunter and clunk from the basement
where my father stoked the morning furnace
by the concrete laundry tub, the coal bin.
The old house coughed up lukewarm air
through baseboard's metal grates.
I dressed fast,
      cold toes clenched on colder lino.
      On my bedroom window, frost flowers.

After school that day
chrysanthemums tapped frozen heads
against the fence
where I leaned my bike.

I let myself in, groped
in the darkening kitchen, blowing
on red knuckles, when,
just perceptibly, the house groaned,
gathered and puckered the air like
skin on scalded milk, like
hair prickling my neck.

Only my father, home early, still
overcoated in the desolate front room,
moaning. My brother dead these six weeks. I
slammed the cocoa tin down
hard as anything and
lit the fire.

★

Odd to find the old place still there.
It stands quiet in the dusk; it seems smaller,
its sensible brown shingles now a heritage palette
of caramel, cobalt, plum,
liquifying through a scrim of mist,
and the first lights coming on.

NASTURTIUMS BRIGHT AND SINUOUS

My friend painted that portrait
above the pine dresser.
Painted me during a long grief,
all bone and gaze,
the strength I'd hoped for.
In silence the brush, its furious motion.
Sharp smells of linseed, turpentine,
and the silver bell of her hair swinging.

A mystery, friendship in a place of loss
and the comfort of an image
made from her own being,
yet which so captured me.

Perhaps they're right, those ancients
who felt a likeness captures the soul.
My other life manifest
through her enlivening eye.

All we might salvage from the dark world.

Later, we laughed a little, poured wine, put on the cello suites,
nasturtiums bright and sinuous in their bowl.

MY SON BATHES HIS FIRSTBORN

Crouched over the tub,
scarred arm steady,
his articulate hand
anchors the small spine.
His coarse hair flops,
veils the belly's soapy gleam.

Feet point a tiny slow ballet.
Bobbly head, its wide gaze.

His free hand soaps and sluices.
He croons and croons.

My whole skin remembers
the silk of him afloat on my arm,
froggy legs languid,
skull-pulse in my elbow-crook,
buttocks narrow in my palm;
the startlement
of his eyes on mine
when we two were the world.

TO MY SON I AM ALIEN

     yet each winter before the year turns,
like the magician who briefly lifts a curse,
he brings me his son
for two days and nights.

We have our rituals.
First, the apple crumble:
my darling how you laugh,
snatch at spiralled apple peels.
     How solemnly you wield the big spoon,
     flour sprinkling around us like a blessing,
     incense of cinnamon, of cloves.

At bedtime, you bring me your wolf book,
knuckle your skull's lovely gourd into my clavicle.

Through blinds, the barred moon.
     Wolves come out of the wall and
     your sweet bones elbow my ribs,
     your gold-dust skin the gift of three continents.

Our fingers trace out words. You breathe round vowels
that fall through the night, sibilant spell
     telling of the striped moon,
        and wolves,
          and the magic boy
           who will vanish
            at daybreak.

DEMETER ABREAST THE WHEAT-RICH MEADOWS

Demeter abreast the wheat-rich meadows
turns only an instant from her beloved,
the child gathering lily and rose,
crocus and violets, narcissus.
Remember the narcissus.

A rift: black plunging horses part tides of wheat
for deathless Hades, his grim reach.
He is not Death, but rules death's sunless realms.
The cleft yawns; vapours thicken, white-armed Persephone
vanishes; her wails thinning into the
downdraft through veins and runnels, sinkholes
harrowing the earth's secret places, and finally
the gates, the ferryman, the five rivers,
fields of asphodel with their despondent shades.

Amongst the grasses, violet and crocus strewn.
Demeter crumbling with grief, crazed,
scavenges earth and heaven for the stolen one,
torches all in her search.
Weak tribes of mortals can inscribe
neither the flat stone of her heart
nor their seed, scorched in the soil's brown furrows.
Her rage is the rage of earth,
its ravage her vengeance.

Finally gods intervene and the girl
emerges into light and air. Her slender feet step through the grass,
her mother races—oh ransomed one, oh beloved—
arms filled with sheaves.

But think of this: who rescued whom? Leaving Hades,
the girl did not refuse the pomegranate.
No longer Kore, maiden, but queen of the underworld, her power
over souls of the dead, over stern Hades' longing
through nights heavy with desire.
She sucks the last juice from the pomegranate seeds.

But the story doesn't end there.

Ever since, its aftermath: terrain scorched and plundered,
Greek theogony defunct. New lords assert *dominion over the earth*;
its treasures, poisoned, smelted, fracked;
an underworld riddled with insult, catacombed
by human craving; a netherworld wracked;
frayed connective tissues of the planet's gathering wrath;
taiga—where, through boreal winter's dark, caribou migrations
rivered the land, flowing to calving grounds,
sky dark with bird multitudes, wings a roar like rapids—
now drifting as oil-clogged remnants on the tailing ponds.

As earth tilts from the sun again
the maiden slips down to her dark lord's embrace.
Even Hades knew his queen would come and
depart in seemly measure as
seasons waxed and waned.

Not we, pomegranate seeds in our mouths.

GLAD IN THE RUTHLESS FURNACE

It's still winter, but a pool of sun simmers
by the garden shed she's painted mauve and rust.
She brings me coffee there, has nailed a cattle skull, horns and all,
under the eaves where a pair of Bewick's wrens scold and trill,
clamber through eye sockets, glean the garden's tangle
to line the cavity of this cupped haven, their nest.

It's like Mrs. Foster told us between treatments,
that on her way back from Costco
she stopped at the funeral home
and paid for her casket with Visa.
Well, why not? she said,
I got enough points for a round trip to Edmonton.

And in the Japanese gardens at Lethbridge,
as summer dark settled on Obon's lanterns
floating toward the lake,
we cast our troubles on those spirits flickering
past the great bronze bell;
the hanging log of its *kanetsuki* vibrated our bone marrow,
and in the background taiko drums
beat our hearts for us.

It's like the poet said,
We must have
the stubbornness to accept our gladness in the ruthless
furnace of this world.
Tears are cheap grace.
Feed your archived grief to the shredder.
     Sometimes a life opens
        to a moment of wind from the sea.

NO PROTOCOL FOR THIS

I

There is no protocol for this, says my poet friend, of a difficult farewell,
those finalities we blunder through
bereft of ceremony. Not even a gold watch, no knell,
no service with its funeral meats
and commiserative gossip.

II

No protocol for the demise of friendship, bereavement deep and lasting
as any blood tie, no extreme unction to mark the end of midnight
sessions laughing or weeping at the kitchen table, private lexicon of
jokes and secrets, finishing the bottle and curling up spooned like sisters
to sleep it off. Then friendship's slow or fast decay: averted eyes, stilted
conversations, the resurrection of small grievances grown monstrous in
their secret lair.

III

And I remember times ago, from our Barbados home, uphill from
sloping cane fields, above a derelict plantation house shabby with history.
A fire had been set, late night; the place went up like tinder, from each
once-grand window a tongue of flame twenty, thirty feet high and
perfectly parallel, a mathematical vision. And then a light wind came up
and they all bent slightly to the north, still perfectly parallel,
parallellagrammed stripes of flame. And over it all, the moon; beyond,
the black black sea. It could have been a David Blackwood etching, only
tropical. Exciting to watch from the porch in the middle of the night,
and even at the time I thought it a fitting metaphor for end of empire.

IV

Nor is there ritual to tell a spouse of many years
that you are leaving. No prescribed decorum.
Nothing was planned.

We were eating lunch on the patio of a mountain restaurant,
cliff forested steeply to the inlet. I said I will die in this life. It struck me
that he could fling me over the rail and I would tumble forever.
I had no map when things fell
into Before and After.

V
Or how to tell people you have cancer? No protocol.
You can keep it to yourself
where it bubbles like porridge, clogging your thoughts so you become a
    bore
and later, inevitably, close friends are hurt you didn't confide. You can

blurt it out
to people in velvet jackets sipping wine at the intermission
so they startle, make polite *mmm* noises
then move carefully away, or

you can toss it off wryly, Oscar-Wilde-ly,
which is a relief to them,
and they say you're handling it really well
and get on with their appointments and shopping, with defrosting the
    fridge.

You can email, which is a bit cowardly,
even vulgar, and reminds me of Mum saying
Don't draw attention to yourself
when I shrugged into that tight red dress.

HER VIRGINIA WOOLF HAT

Last wash of sun across the bookcase
strokes my cousin's photograph. She is laughing
under her Virginia Woolf hat,
     turning from garden to camera.

We were both laughing. I'd opened another bottle.
We argued happily about supper—cook or use leftovers?
     The day replete, shadowless.

We knew nothing of the proliferating cells
that would kill her
before the next year was out.

Look behind her: the grasses are lush
and shoulder-high, the peonies luxuriant,
their fleshy petals weighty
among bosky shrubs.

Evening now. The room dims, and the photograph.
Still she turns to me laughing.

That preposterous hat.

DISAMBIGUATION

You sat watching the insect kingdom's advance directives
in your garden. Brambled overgrowth knitting itself
like malign hedges in fairy tales. No rescuers in sight.
    In your armchair almost to the end, ginger cat in your lap.
    Your hair fluff grown back, a dandelion.

But sister-cousin, you were gold and leggy in our salad days.
We outwitted parents, sprinted from their dull lifescapes.

In Switzerland we ate spring asparagus.

You, younger with your child's-cry of *not fair, not fair.*

No, not fair. Your long dying, the cells that ate you.
    Your rage at rumpled tea towels, crumbs in the toaster.
        Betrayals I should have foreseen.

I long for the simplicity of pure sorrow.
    My mother for instance: such good company she was!
    Bittersweet to pass her clapboard house, her blackberries.

Not foreverness of the unresolvable.
Not indeterminacy of resentment. Grief.

Here is a new word: *disambiguation.*
See me now, tightrope walker. I toe the line, maintaining balance,
    attentive to biomechanics—tricky at times.
    Expecting anything as the world unfolds below,
      spacious
          and promising uncertainty.
            The huge cloud-piled sky.

ALL SOULS

Late October rain drains
to the year's darker half.
Gunmetal sky drips through ferns and shrubs; their roots
reach down toward the quiet creep
of small crawling things.
Maple leaves gold and dying
and the veil between two worlds so permeable I do believe
the dead will drift in on this scrim of rain,
and beckon us or stare sadly.

How to greet them?
The beloved cousin dying enraged and full of blame.
Grandmother, wringing her hands.
Would the teacher we tormented still choke on chalk dust?
Memories run red, return to me.
My sad brother in a far place shattering his life.
And murdered pupils I taught once half a world away—
brother and sister, from the school pageant they two-stepped
into the night. Oh they were flaming and frail.
That night their mother set their room ablaze.
Would they come to me dancing?
Would their small charred limbs point and tremble?

I shop for groceries with
the Eritrean woman from my language class,
point out pumpkins, bales of hay, kids decked out
like fairies, cowboys, little pirates.
Then mirrored in her eyes
see shelves of knife-embedded skulls, plastic brains,
gore-splattered casts of severed hands and feet
right in the supermarket, and in her eyes

that veil between the worlds so torn
that all her dreadful dead
come climbing through.

A CURRICULUM OF TEA

The young teacher heats a kettle
in the small-town high school
where prairie winds splat gritty snow
against windows while he pours tea
for his Babel class, boys who spar in seven languages.
       All children of war well-versed
       in curses, fists, knives;
they whet their skills on one another.

He has searched anarchy for a binding
and found they all drink tea.

For an hour each morning they circle chairs,
       slouch and murmur as he pours
       from one boy to the next. They cup their hands,
       breathe coiling steam, breathe respite.

WAVE AND PARTICLE

We are gleaners who fill
the barn for the winter that comes on.
  —Jack Gilbert, "Moreover"

Stars: already we see only their memory, yet our senses
bear witness to a swirling van Gogh glory.
Lying in a summer night's grass, who would not
be drawn along that huge current?

The gathering in of thresholds,
an unceasing dance, annihilation and creation;
even as subatomic particles collide
new particles are born, Wu Li dancing masters.

I remember tunnelled waves of labour, their cramp and release,
that small particle of life unfurling, tiny hands and mouth
avid; in decades he too will gather himself in
surrender to the cosmos. And late

in winter dusk,
ice on the roadside pond,
we drove from the river valley, a steep ascent,
on one side the hill almost a cliff,
and from the scruff of winter grass, slight movement—
deer, at least twenty under the sickle moon,
all kneeling in the hillside's small hollows
like earth's avatars, night's familiars,
the delicate leaves of their ears
and their great eyes
turned to our headlights' slow passing. It was

pure animal nature looking out from that hill.
What inhabits the body's machinery, opposing entropy?
The moon, the hill, the gaze, our receiving of it—
Which is wave, which particle?
What witness, the patient stones?

INTO THE LAND OF YOUR BODY

Miraculous how skin touches a world
that beckons all the senses,
that deciphers the runes of your body.
Look closely. Look till you have to turn away,
just when you have your questions ready
and your parents are gone.
If you move quickly you might find them
peering down the bannister to see you're home safely,
or folding sheets flat, smoothing them,
or stacking dishes quietly.
Something just in the corner of an eye,
gone when you swivel but there in the mirror,
inhabiting your face
so you step

out of time,
into another world where you find
missing pieces
the atlas left out:
something carnivorous
in unlit rooms: here be dragons.
But go down to rescue the dead;
find her face in the mirror, in the deep well of your heart
as you drop in coins of your thought. They will bring you home
then, to the budding flame bush,
skydiving hummingbirds, the violence of spring
and its intransigent burgeoning.
From even the cold and dark times, remember
breathing a peephole through frost
damasking winter windows.

UNFOLDING

The work of existence devours its own unfolding.
—Jane Hirshfield, "Like an Ant Carrying Her Bits of Leaf or Sand"

The trowel has almost disintegrated,
its scoop frangible, pocked with rust.
    Knocked, it rings like an empty bucket,
    its smell a memory of rain.

    Its shale and spall greet air and water,
    return, ferrous, to their birth from the earth's veins.

Its blade's curve seems less an artifact,
more the Fibonacci swoop of a corroded nautilus.

Half its handle gone, remnant
pinned by a rusted stub of grommet,
fungal filaments, beetle-riddled as though calved
    from lichen-coated nursery logs
        felled by winter storms.

    I thought you'd want it, said my cousin.
    I found it in her compost heap.

Something ancient. Its corrosion surely longer
than the time of her forgetting.

When it rested in its plainness among tools,
    sturdy handle ringed with yellow paint,
      we sat on the back step shelling peas in an enamel colander.
        She gave us the big kitchen spoon to play gardening,
        held buttercups under our chins.

because he cannot remember
how to arrange placemats on the table.
He lays a careful line of kibble
across the floor. It is the tow rope.
If only he could reach the chairlift
he would rise singing.
He would play his violin on the summit;
its high arpeggios become
the screeling voices of anoraked children
in the winter park swinging and swinging
the cold afternoon, till he walks the morning beach
opening oysters with his penknife. He pays the scrambling child
a penny for each oyster she brings; she laughs,
mock horror as he slurps them down.
Then the woman on his porch brings two cold beers
and they sit with their feet on the railing
watching her brown boys tumble the garden.
They call him Grandad, clamour for his jokes and card tricks.

Down here, tormentors hide his shoes,
make him count backwards by sevens.
Where is his violin?
Who took away the boys?
They have flung all his goodness into the fiery furnace.

The chairlift, unstopping, disappears in the mist.
Along the road, the windows of houses
stare out through chestnut trees.

CONSIDER THE HEART AND ITS BREAKING

A hollow fist-sized muscle, an incessant
knock on the door of our lives—
whether in love or terror,
ennui or tranquility.
Its receiving galleries set the beat of our breath,
our passion's pulse and cling,
and the long sleep after.

Buddhists have one word for heart-mind.

Mammals, we have fully divided hearts, two pumps.
Fully divided. We know this well:
The heart is deceitful above all things, and desperately wicked,
says the Book. But with heartbreak our two-ness splits, falls apart,

our woe bypasses reason, hijacks self-respect,
leaks through Vivaldi's adagios and the radio's hurtin' songs,
sobs abjectly.

Heartbreak, intransitive, parses the body,
puts on old clothes I thought had gone to Oxfam.

Longing's soundscape is ecstasy's simulacrum;
its cadence moaning *oh, oh, oh,*
and stretching vowels: *alienate, ache, crave.*

Consider whales' hearts, car-sized.
You could somersault in them.
How to imagine their unfathomable longing;
the massive adagio of their briny lust
must roll down ocean trenches,

cross latitudes,
fill the abyss.

Envy the hummingbird the tiny berry of its savage heart.

METAMORPHOSIS

They have said goodbye to their boy on his slab
and now they wake early,
wait for a slammed fridge, for too-loud music.

Grief's ambush lurks in the laundry basket,
skulks behind cereal boxes, swivels on hinges.
Surely that was a creak on the stairs.

Their friend the potter is early in her studio.
She will make his urn.
She will blend his ashes with the clay-body
and wedge it to complete malleability.
Under her fingers the spinning clay
will rise as though breathing,
move up and out, curve to a form
of perfect repose,
gyre from its still centre.

It must dry. Utterly.
Even tears that fell on it
must return to the air.
In the kiln it will glow
and harden for the ages.

And when his mother holds it
she will hold his bones in her arms.

THE GORGE SUITE: A CARTOGRAPHY OF SORROWS

I. A Hole Four Hundred Years Deep

The neighbouring building: a Mondrian of windows—
some glowing, some dim or dark—
reaches high into the night. Late
for those cubed and layered lives
bathed in television's blue glow, or
spotlighted leafing through magazines, or
silhouetted, shades drawn
(perhaps ghosts who wander rooms
or whistle tunelessly, making cocoa).

Later, more windows darken. A frenetic wind
shreds the cloud cover. The full moon blazing,
its yellow nimbus baleful, swelling the tides.
Windows now opaque hold darkness in,
cloak sleepers in silence.
One shaded square glows where, perhaps,
someone, sleepless, fitfully reads in bed,
shaded lamp turned from a sleeping partner.

★

Down between the canyon of our buildings
the Gorge threads in from the Salish Sea;
its skin, black and glistening, swallows the city's lights,
flexes the ancient muscle of its tides
hauling the sea inland.
Some mornings I look down at treetops; the last gold leaves
float a ceiling of mist, a milky flood
spilling from the sea,
its edges incandescent from a sun
faint as a pale pewter penny.

Coils of fog shift and heave up the Gorge
like another tide, blanket the town, and it's easy
                              to imagine that bulging current
            surging up the inlet and, emerging from the fog,
            wooden canoes, murmur of voices, Lekwungen.
            Perhaps children crouched amid the paddlers, silent,
            their Nefertiti heads delicate as cameos.
            The waterway held sacred places and who knows
            what shape-shifting, human or animal, among living and dead.

★

On still mornings I have kayaked
the bird sanctuary where gulls, ducks, geese, herons
have squabbled in the shallows for centuries,
            where the sky mirrors its blessing on the water,
            where I paddle past the contaminated soil dump,
                  its slopes grasped by rugosa, broom, wild sweet pea,
                  fretwork of gulls along the ridge.

            How the old ones' presence inhabits this place:
            trading up the inlets or sometimes
            crossing open sea as far as Sooke
            before autumn gales set in.
            The T'Sou-ke eager for trade.
            Canoes heaped, dried bulbs harvested
            from camas meadows sloping to the sea. Some remain;

late in spring their blossoms flow and ripple like another sky,
momento mori that this fine condo rises
from a hole four hundred years deep.

II. Cracker Boxes for the Children

Raven, ancient watcher. Creaking pinions
trace his flight above the inlet.
The Narrows dangerous at full tide. Then

past gravel pits and shipyard, a bird sanctuary
and a small rocky island, once a boundary
between Coast Salish clans; also

an island of the dead. Here carved memorial figures
held burial boxes, loved ones curled, fetal,
and at twilight the bereaved paddled out

with sap torches, food for the dead,
chanted long into the night. Then changing times, trade:
travelling trunks used as coffins, wooden cracker boxes

for the children. On this placid June day
the Olympic Range's ice-cream peaks sparkle
while cyclists click across the trestle bridge,

kayakers drift on the tide,
and swallows dart to nesting boxes.
Raven watchful on the railing.

Low tide and the islet ringed with tidemarks.
A cartography of sorrows.

III. *Sakura, Sakura*

Winter has been harsh
with catarrh and grief.

Such quiet across the bridge
where first light streaks the night-tide
and early cherry blossoms embroider the dark.

Clouds are limned with light.
Small sounds of coughing
and rattle of the homeless man's cart
from bushes behind the market.
The froth of blossom overhead
scatters petals, an eagle-down blessing,
as it has done since 1938
when cherry saplings lined the streets. *Sakura, sakura,*
a gift from the Japanese community.
Two years later, enemy aliens,
broken blossoms strewn across a floating world. *Ukiyo-e.*

Petals as clouds:
they are that ephemeral, that intense.
Whether spring grace, whether diaspora,
timely, untimely, all things rise and pass away.
Despite sandwich lunches, socks rolled in drawers,
the beloved child is lost.
When my friend gathered her son's ashes, she said,
Now he weighs about the same
as when I first brought him home.

How we crave the more-ness of the lovely
while petals brocade the boulevards
                    and fall on our upturned faces.

IV. Tides

A moonless chill promised frost
as we walked home across the blue bridge, when
two, three, then four sculls slid out along the black water,
each with a light on its prow, not a flambeau,
although it flickered like flame, mirrored and shimmered
adagio in the dark over the outgoing tide, doubled stars a coruscation
under the westward moving river of heaven
and we, elated, hurried home to each other's arms—
currents of our veins, their tributaries—to unknow
for a while how all things under heaven
are dragged about, tidal,
even the spring and neap of our own lives, or

that a tide of young women in their loveliness and in their hundreds
has flowed along that Highway we call Tears,
disappeared or washed up as flotsam
as predictably as the earth turning on its great spindle
drags its cloaks of shining water, or to unknow

that, seen from the air, the drift and set
of people moving
has a certain organic elegance as they flow, Nigerian, Syrian
towards boundaries, and how, like a tidal bore,
military waves crest to send a stronger edge

and finding myself among strangers at a party,
adrift amongst the canapés,
I made small talk with a clever man, mannerly,
an anaesthetist. And when asked, I rashly said, *I'm a poet.*
His handsome face composed itself, a slack tide changing direction
when he said, *You know, I've never been able*
to get my head around that kind of thing.

V. O Heron, My Familiar

Drifting from the trestle's barnacled shade,
my kayak flushes a heron
who lifts, blocks the sun
        so its seraphim wings blaze,
          so its ballerina feet glow,
            so its shadow feathers my hull.

VI. Solstice

It is the way of shadow to heap
in louring clouds
along the berserk tilt of the earth.

It is the way of dark to feed our lust
for the luminous, so we begrudge
a sullen smudge of light smeared on the world's rim
and even *that* diminishing, bedraggled as homeless men
hunched in moonless doorways.

It is the way of night
to winch tides in its wake
till darkness saturates, floods night's meniscus
      and, like an unspooling bolt of grey silk,
        a swell of current pushes along the inlet,
          snow geese breasting the tide.
Soon there will be snow.

Yet the year's fulcrum once more pauses,
shifts toward light.
          It is the way of light
to ripen us; our daguerreotype lives lift,
polished on silvered surfaces of travail.

A HEART, FOOLISH HERMENEUT

Watch from the coulee's scoured edge—
a hot wind bristles its scruffy pelt.
Marvel that anything fluid
could so burrow the valley,
could so insinuate that gleaming celadon curl.

Walk the river's edge
where scrub and root entangle overhead
and wedge the astonished trees
with winter's roil and floodwrack.

Suspended
over the river's drift,
a flotilla of white pelicans
floats the air.

A heart, foolish hermeneut,
could open to their floppity grace;
could yearn after that unlikely green current
threading archeologies of loss;
could imagine it to be more
than its meandering
tough
geographical
self.

THEY HAVE TAKEN AWAY MY GOOD MIRRORS

I

       these three: heart–sisters all, dead in one year.

One, my custodian of guilty pleasures: tucked in flannel sheets
we watched *What Not to Wear*. Her transparent hands.

Another read me her poems while she could,
told me her husband would blame me.

Oh madcaps, wordsmiths, who will remember
the corkscrew? Who will finish my sentences? Where will I go?

Fog blots the evening, dilutes destinations. Mist coating my cheeks.
I fall into dreams of void and absence.

It is time to furnish the hiatus. A course, perhaps. A book club.
Spring bulbs for the balcony, papery in the cold soil.

II
My tall son, radiant with rage,
has stalked off down a different road.

A late wasp thrums the window.

The downy pulse of his skull, his mango skin.

Cumbersome heart: it creaks open like an old travelling trunk
stuffed with this burdensome love;

can't hold it gingerly between my two palms
as I might hold your face.

III

I'm on the no-fly list. Graceless times, twelve-year-old Olivers in the
    stockroom.
A homeless man puts his head on my shoulder, says, *I'm so lonely.*

Street lights stutter in the rain. All evening
the city's starveling hopes gather in doorways.

Behind scaffolding, like dorm boys after lights out,
men in sleeping bags and plastic read by flashlight.

A moon like the ring a glass leaves on varnish.

THAT SUMMER BAY WHEN SORROW WAS A CHILD

and crows cawed the arbutus dawn. Evenings
you held frilled oyster shells against the sunset,
mother-of-pearl glowing into your small world.

Mornings you sculled the shallows
raking up huge pre-pollution crabs,
a world all salt and mist, your mother calling breakfast,
and at dusk crabs scuttled,
made a wheezing sound
with their scrabble, brief, in water
boiling on the campfire
where you cracked them open with such gusto,
sucked out the meat.
           Your father's corny jokes
and the world lurching on,
its spoor tucked in mouldy boxes, newspapers
stacked by the old coal bin. Albums, their black pages curating
a scowling childhood. Your older cousins squint into the sun,
recall only boredom of dusty days
without romance, tedium of chores,
parents a fretful backdrop. What matter
they wore themselves threadbare
over the mortgage and wondered
        where the lick and flare of passion,
        what that small lump fingered in the dark.

You just want to put your head on the desk.

But you held giggling parliaments,
rubbed baby oil on peeling shoulders,
scorned your mother's gifts of soft pink sweaters.

Then read of Emmett Till. Just your age, fourteen—
he whistled at a white woman.
Battered, barbwired to a flywheel, thrown in the Mississippi.
His mother made them leave his coffin open.
Let the world see what happened, she said.

So the world's Boschian maw, insatiable,
        intractable,
gaped before your green life.
Retreat impossible.

Did you think you could go back?

Words like *love* and *justice* less than tidewrack on the beach
        even if you could find that oyster shell,
                hold it against the light.

NEVERTHELESS, SHE PLANTS THE BULBS

Windless chill on the sun-patched balcony.
Soft and cold in its heavy bag, potting soil
to drag and scoop and tamp down over bulbs—
crocus, snowdrop—their papery rustling skins
pressed deep in the quiet dark
to await the year's turning,
to promise waves of colour
in an unimaginable spring.

Only an October sun, layering the sedum,
and heuchera glowing chartreuse.
Only the last bees dying,
one crawling into the brass bowl,
one butting against the pane,
its shadow breathing on my arm.

NIGHT WIND

Night wind, an erratic pendulum,
slaps pulsing rain
against the glass.
Lamplight slants
its cone of light, a small aurora borealis,
through the black pane.
The woman surfaces—
an aureole of stuttering light
limns the cranium, mandible, sockets,
dissolves soft ropes of flesh.
How did she drown, that sparky girl,
her verve in the storm,
wet laughing face turned to the sky?
With morning, the rain-clean patio gleams.
Finches a cappella on the placid tiles.

Finches a cappella on the placid tiles
in the morning. The rain-clean patio gleams.
Her wet laughing face turned to the sky,
her verve in the storm—
what drowned that sparky girl,
dissolved soft ropes of flesh
that limned the cranium, mandible, sockets?
Amid aureoles of stuttering light
the woman surfaces
in the black pane.
Its cone of light a small aurora borealis,
lamplight slants
against the glass,
stipples rain's pulse; slaps of
night wind, an erratic pendulum.

MEETING AN OLD FRIEND IN BANFF, AUTUMN

Nights are cooler now. Winds slide down mountains,
flake the aspens' first gold.

Sunlight is cancelled early; Rundle's ridgelines
shoulder the light aside. A last flare mottles
the peaks, their scattered pelts of lodgepole pine, spruce,
patchy shale.

Stranger than any creation story:
seas rising to mountaintop reefs,
collecting spalls in muddy maelstroms
dumped randomly, heaving up ziggurats
along the spiny continental massif,
weathering into vegetation. Stranger than

doctrines of *ex nihilo*, things brought into being by naming;
than the Greek myth of Chaos, populated by incestuous gods;
of tales of Raven, prankish light-bringer.

What purpose this machinery?
What meaning for our mayfly lives?

Are crags and outcrops more real if
I say *Mesozoic*, rather than
The moon climbs into autumn?

Far from home I meet an old friend.
Kindred spirits rare, I should know by now.
We pour wine, laugh a little.
Tomorrow we will walk by the river;

its unravelling streams braid dark and light.
Magpies startle, glide on sudden gusts.
Any morning now there will be frost.

ON LOOKING INTO DAVID BLACKWOOD'S SEASCAPES

Wax resist on a copper plate
repels the nitric acid, vinegar-sharp,
but the etching needle seeks that icy void,
presses down to its core; the acid bites and bites
like the iceberg pressing through the skin of the world,
its vaults and pinnacles gleaming in the night.
Trapped starlight refracts sheen and spangle and

plunges down searoads winding like rope
through upside-down mountains, peaks and chasms
where fish-huddles stream, silver, mouths agape;
their round sleepless eyes glint into the dark, the dark,
and through it all, leviathans surge,
the huge bell of their song.

There is no end to their longing.

Above, small hunters in white sealskin coats. Their sliver of boat
threads night water, rippling silence,
and over the iceberg three seabirds
wing—the hollow crick crick of their flight
under the resinous moon.

VERROCCHIO'S ANGEL

Terracotta bas-relief, severe, serene:
descending in a whirl of holy wind, Verrocchio's angel;
    his great wings' thrust and flex,
        tilt and camber.
Their beating comes to me in dreams,
soars through time and space from the great quattrocento campanile
to this coast, its meaning insistent but indecipherable
      above matted rosehips, late blackberries, manic small birds,
      flattened grass where the homeless sometimes shelter.

That thick fir slab I've saved,
    grain paralleled so fine it will print
      a windless day's gentlest rain.

My scapular muscles twitch, empathic
to translate winged flight: drawings, washes.
Then inked on fir, thumb-smoothed.
    My small arsenal neatly arrayed:
      gouges, knives, chisels.
      A whetstone.

Image now locked in the wood grain
and in the mind's eye.
Now. Carve out negative space
    gouge nestled against right palm,
    pushing, braked by the left.

The world falls away.
Fine emptiness
of a late hour. Only the desk lamp
breathing its light across a wood-chip cairn.
    The old masters visit: Hiroshige, Hokusai. Lines thin as hairs.

Once my right hand slipped, a V-gouge through my left palm.
A relief it was only my mendable hand,
not an engraved edge, irreversibly splintered.

Coffee. Stretch. Brush off every wood chip.
On the immaculate desk
a finished woodblock and fine rice paper, thick.
    Now comes the roller's sticky rhythm—schlip schlip—
    inking its perfect film into the block's pores
       as forest fires gone underground
          smoulder along coal seams, waiting
             to burst forth like revelation.

Paper aligned and burnished, every inch.
Breath held. Paper held,
corners slowly peeled away: the first proof, arm's-length.
The mystery of making.
    The making imperfect but whole.
      In my head a rushing wind
      and the sound of wings
        beating.

WHAT WE FEEL MOST HAS NO NAME

It's on the tip of my tongue, I say,
when, as in dreams, meanings dart like fingerlings
through the net of my intentions.

What word, precise and elegant,
for the gestures
of Thai temple dancers?
Or the way my mother's face
swims to my morning mirror?

Is it only with peripheral vision
that the Kore's Archaic smile evokes mystery?
Servant of the temple,
is she blessed by gods
or just pleased to be liberated from stone?

Do the silver nutmeg and golden pear
encode heart's desire?

The infant's world–making gaze
harvests no words.

How dreadfully the dead boy's morticianed face
denotes the final silence.

What we feel most has no name
but *maelstrom, finchsong, sundial,*

constellation.

INSOMNIA'S GIFTS

The night unpacks its dark hours slowly,
pulls the moon down my west window,
slides a moonlight lozenge along the floor.

Night's not always phantomed with regrets.
Insomnia's gift's a night-world I inhabit alone,
a settling of mind
as of a body settling into quilts,
as of opposite windows sheltering
sleepers turning slow as swimmers
into their dreams.

Humming, the building breathes its warmth
down dream-crowded corridors, shadows
drifting door to door, poems in their pockets,
and it seems
for me alone; how the moon scuds
as though through torn lace;
wind's buffeting, faint;
a passing cab's susurration on wet streets,

and in the corner, stolid shadow cubes:
pine dresser, slab of shelf,
air thickening its wavering edges.
What has vanished can yet be known
in the clarifying day.

FOUR TIMES I HAVE ENTERED THE COUNTRY OF WORDS

To change your language you must change your life.
            —Derek Walcott, "Codicil"

Childhood's fief: I perched oblivious
on a continent's edge crusting
above the Cascadia fault.
Hid in ferns and cedars,
hollered down beaches, their cobbled click and grate.

Kelp-scribbled
leviathan driftwood, whorled
snouts gnarled and knobbed.

And I hovered on barnacled knees over rock-pool kingdoms
of ravenous anemones, nacreous shells
that mirrored my upside-down self.

★

Caribbean decades, margins shifting. Look out
from any beach:
no landfall, only horizon.
That young woman on the far shore of my years
learning to know herself as
other, the vowels
of her mouth growing
languorous with patois.
At Accra Beach her sons glowed gold, suspended
in cresting waves, translucent.

★

Mid-life I Rip-Van-Winkled back
to shifting boundaries, Pacific shores, old kingdoms gone,
unspiced food, drivers on the wrong side of the road,

and a Canadian accent repossessed my mouth,
my pale face emptied the mirror;
my face, paler.

★

In my fourth age you heard the words of my heart.
I left my life. Lost my sons.
I called across the riptides of their loss
but they did not hear me,
nor did they care to.
Thrust into a new sphere,
I rummage beaches,
find flotsam's fringes, thresholds,
changing my language to change my life.

THOUGH ALL THINGS IN A DREAM BE EQUAL

The woman wakes to an unreal bed, shuffles into fuzzy slippers.
           Stands at the night window
           as if she has entered a painting by Hopper.

As if a theatre curtain has opened.

As if a woman's wail is counterpoint
           to the passing siren.

As if the black gleaming streets
           blinking go-stop-go-stop signify
           grace.

Along the street where shadows shift in boutique doorways,
           a cigarette glows, arcs.
           The shadows hunch and settle,
inhabit the city's troubled dream.

Though all things in a dream be equal,
           not these:
neither the woman cursing and sobbing on the corner
nor the one at the window.
She is sipping hot chocolate.

Notes

Pu Ru Paints Zhong Kui the Demon Queller on a Mule

Pu Ru (1896–1963) was an artist and calligrapher in the classical tradition, and was cousin to the last Emperor of China. He retreated to a monastery in the Western mountains to avoid the era's political upheavals.

At the Barbados Museum

In Barbados, dengue fever is called bone-brek fever.

Manumission was the complex and expensive legal process through which an enslaved person could be reclassified as free.

Port of Spain is the capital of Trinidad.

In the Galaxy of Our Eyes

A tribute to my drawing teacher Glenn Howarth (1946-2009), who taught me not to believe the evidence of my eyes.

The fovea, a small pit at the back of the eye, is responsible for sharp acuity of vision. Although it covers only the central 2% of visual field, it takes up over 50% of the visual cortex.

Praise-Song for Jenny

The first two lines of this poem are from Barbara Colebrook Peace's "Song of God: The night before you were born" in *Duet for Wings and Earth*.

Late and the Light Already Turning

Title and its repetition are from John Berger's *Once in Europa*.

A Fibonacci Sequence

Fibonacci (c. 1170–1250) was an Italian mathematician who sought perfection of proportion in art and nature through a mathematical sequence of numbers. Related to the Golden Mean of the ancient Greeks, a Fibonacci sequence goes: 0, 1, 1, 2, 3, 5, 8, 13, 21, 34 and so forth. Each number is the sum of the two preceding numbers. In this poem, the number of words in each line follows a Fibonacci sequence.

Feeding Poets

When the poet Pamela Porter attends Patrick Lane's poetry retreats, she arrives with a large tin of Mexican wedding cakes. Those who bite into these delectable and addictive golf-ball-sized sweets, find themselves showered with a spray of sugary crumbs.

How It All Gathers

netsuke: A traditional Japanese button or toggle-like ornament on a kimono cord, usually intricately carved in wood or ivory.
miyabi: A Japanese aesthetic ideal, usually translated as elegant, refined, polished, and graceful.

Glad in the Ruthless Furnace

The title and italicized lines are from Jack Gilbert's "A Brief for the Defence," from *Refusing Heaven*: "We must have/the stubbornness to accept our gladness in the ruthless/furnace of this world."
kanetsuki: The wooden log-like ringer swung against the side of a large bell.

No Protocol for This

The title is from an unpublished poem by Grace Cockburn.

Into the Land of Your Body

The title is from a line in Giles Benaway's *Land of the Dead*.

The Gorge Suite

A Hole Four Hundred Years Deep
The title and its repetition are from Ursula Vaira's "Sweat Lodge" in
The Journey Poems.
their Nefertiti heads: Noble families among the Coast Salish traditionally
bound the heads of their infants into an aristocratic loaf-like shape.

Cracker Boxes for the Children
Hacklett Island, a small rocky islet by the Selkirk Trestle in Victoria's
Gorge Inlet, was traditionally a burial ground for the local Songhees
people.

Sakura, Sakura
Sakura are cherry blossoms. In 1938 the Japanese-Canadian commu-
nity of Victoria won the city's Victoria Day parade prize for the best
float. They used the prize money to provide Victoria with plantings of
cherry trees that still flourish on the citys' boulevards. Two years later
they were declared enemy aliens and their property confiscated.
Ukiyo-e is the "floating world" of Japanese art, peaking in the 17th and
18th centuries, but influential into modern times. Printmakers and art-
ists brought to their art a sense of the brevity and inevitable passing of
pleasure, beauty, the seasons, and life itself.

Meeting an Old Friend in Banff, Autumn
The italicized lines are from *The Mountain Poems of Meng Hao-jin*,
translated by David Hinton (Archipelago Books, 2004).

What We Feel Most Has No Name
This poem is after Jack Gilbert's "The Forgotten Dialect of the Heart"
(from *The Great Fires*).

Acknowledgements

My gratitude to the editors of periodicals where several of these poems have appeared: *Arc Poetry Magazine, Room Magazine, Island Writer Magazine, Prairie Fire, Freefall*, and *Plenitude Magazine*. Poems have also appeared in Patrick Lane's annual retreat chapbooks, and been anthologized in *Poems from Planet Earth* (Leaf Press, 2013), *The Wild Weathers: A Gathering of Love Poems* (Leaf Press, 2012), and *Walk Myself Home: an anthology to end violence against women* (Caitlin Press, 2010). I have also recast several poems from my own chapbooks: *Sliding Towards Equinox* (Rubicon Press, 2009), *Those Astonishments of Sorrow, of Joy* (Leaf Press, 2012), and *The Gorge: A Cartography of Sorrows* (JackPine Press, 2016).

Since 2007, I have profited from Patrick Lane's astute and generous mentorship, and among his poetry retreat participants, I have found my tribe. Love and gratitude to you all.

Thanks to Russell Thorburn, shaper of manuscripts, who first sorted my heap of poems into a unified whole. I am deeply thankful for thoughtful and constructive insights of Pamela Porter and Arleen Paré, who critiqued subsequent drafts.

It is a pleasure to acknowledge the Banff Centre's excellent writing programs, where I worked with Patrick Friesen, Don Domanski, and Don McKay. I encountered Don McKay again at Sage Hill Writing Experience, where his meticulous eye and his encouragement guided my final honing of this manuscript.

At Brick Books, I am grateful for Kitty Lewis's friendly and practical overview, and for Barry Dempster's warm engagement and incisive editorial vision. Thanks also to Production Manager Alayna Munce, maestra of clarity, nuance, and grammar.

My collective noun: a kindness of poets.

Thank you Leah, for love, support, and encouragement.

WENDY DONAWA, formerly a college instructor and museum curator in Barbados, now lives and writes in Victoria. Her poems have appeared in several Canadian anthologies and literary journals, and in her three chapbooks, most recently with JackPine Press. *Thin Air of the Knowable* is her debut collection.